Parents:

Learning to tell time is an exciting achievement for children. They can tell when it's time for mother and/or father to get home from work, when their favorite television programs are on, when it's time to leave for a special outing, etc. It is a skill we take for granted since we learned how to do it so long ago. Some children find it easier to learn than others. Be patient and provide opportunities for your child to find out what time it is. The activities in this book will help you and your child reach this goal.

Go on a "Clock Search" (page 2)

Walk around the house with your child. Have him/her point out all the places that tell time. Point out places your child overlooks such as the clock on the microwave oven or the VCR. Have your child draw the timepieces he/she finds on page 2 of this book.

Make a paper plate clock (page 3)

You will need to provide your child with these items to use in making a clock face:

- 2 paper plates (or a cardboard circle and some scraps)
- a large paper fastener
- scissors
- glue
- sharp pencil

Steps to follow:

1. If your child can use scissors, have him/her cut out the clock face and the hands on page 3. If not, cut the pieces out yourself.

2. Help your child glue the clock face to one paper plate and the hands to the second paper plate. After the glue has dried, cut the hands out again (the paper plate will give them added strength).

3. Use the pencil to poke a hole in the clock and hands where marked with a small circle. You will need to do this for your child.

4. Place the hands on the clock face and attach them with the paper fastener. Move the hands around a few times to be sure they are moving freely.

Your child will need this clock several times while doing the activities in this book.

Parents: Read the directions for a clock search on page 1.

I'm Going on a Clock Search

Parents: Read the directions on page 1 for making this clock.

My Own Clock

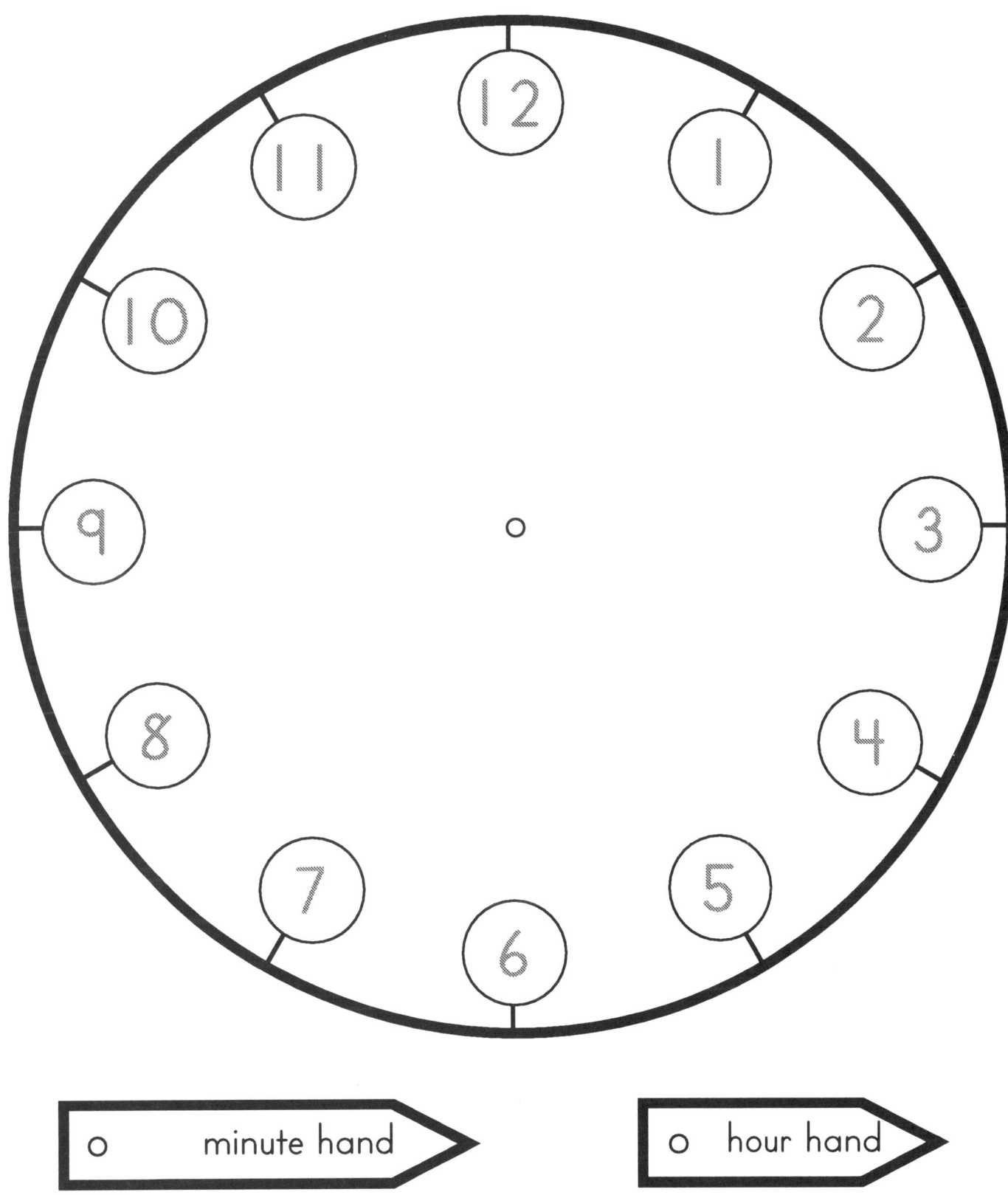

Parents: Point out to your child that the clock front is called the face and that the pieces that move around are called hands.

Color the Hands

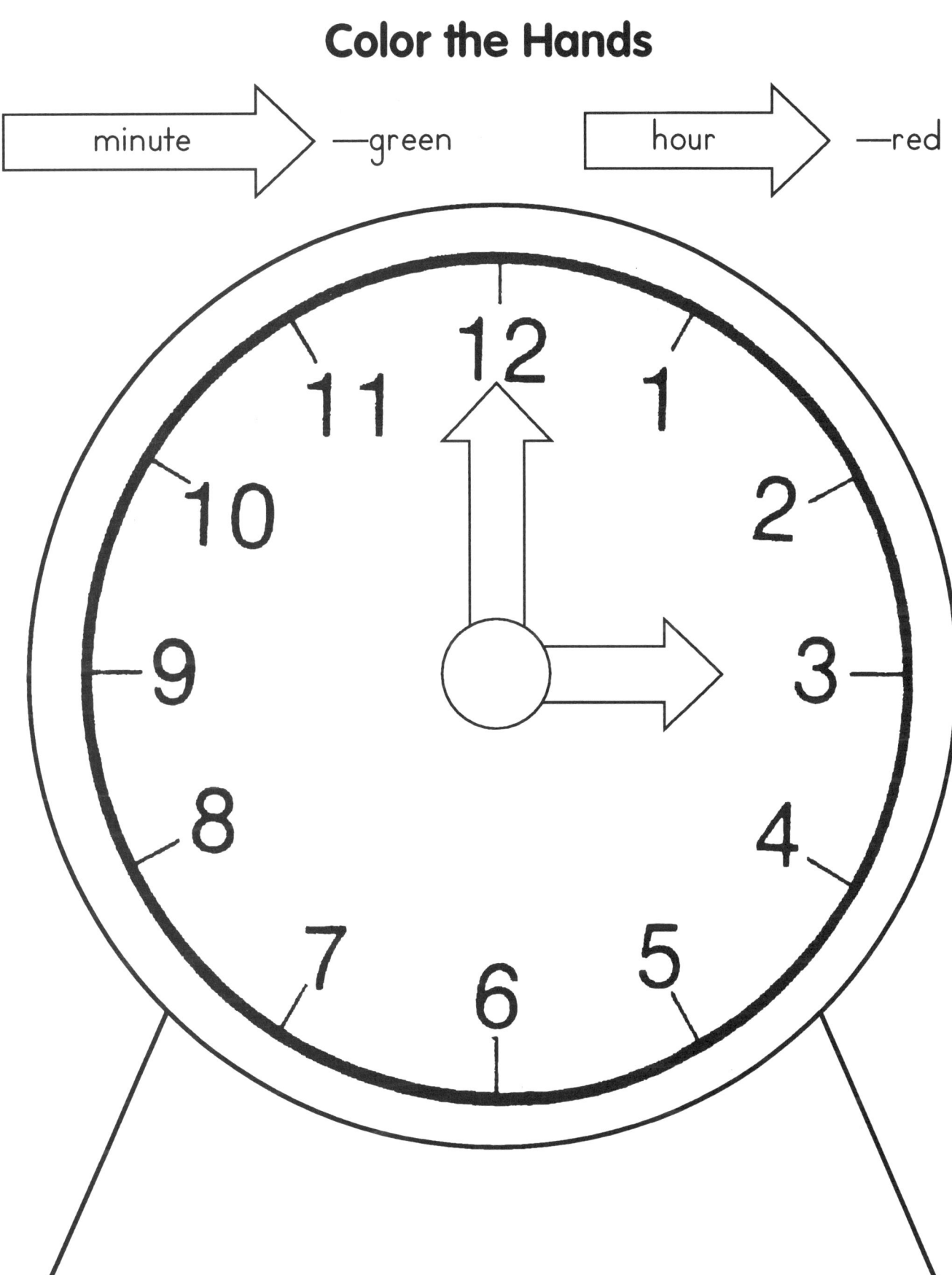

minute → —green

hour → —red

Parents: Explain to your child that when the big hand is on the 12, we look at the little hand to see what hour it is. Practice with the paper plate clock, having your child put the long hand on the 12 and the little hand pointing to each number in turn. Have him/her say "It is 3 o'clock ." and so on as the little hand is moved. Then look at the clocks on this page. Have your child tell you the hour.

What time is it?

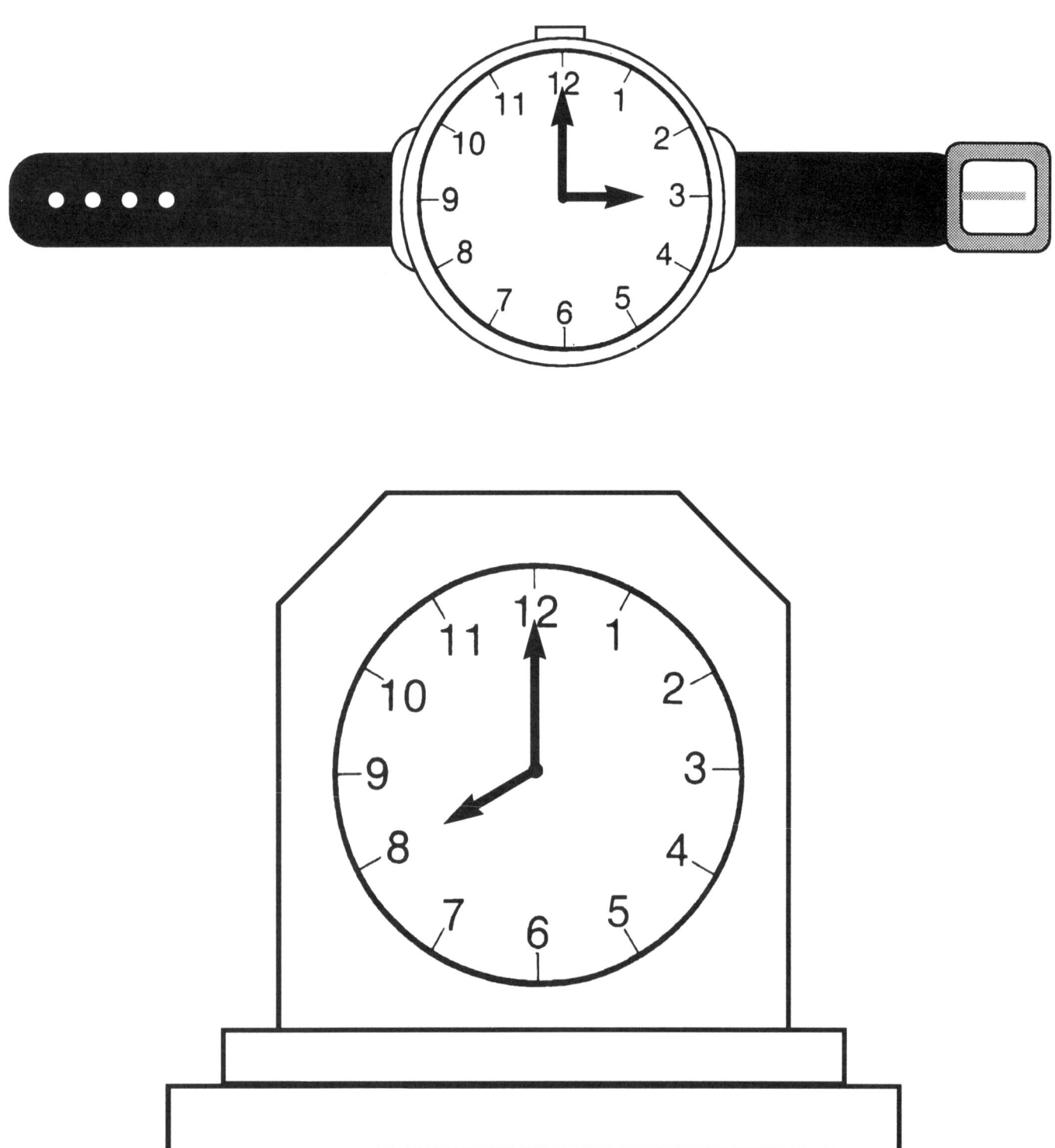

What time is it?

Circle the time.

(7 o'clock) 4 o'clock

8 o'clock (5 o'clock)

2 o'clock 4 o'clock

8 o'clock 10 o'clock

3 o'clock 6 o'clock

9 o'clock 1 o'clock

What time is it?

Match the clock to the hour.

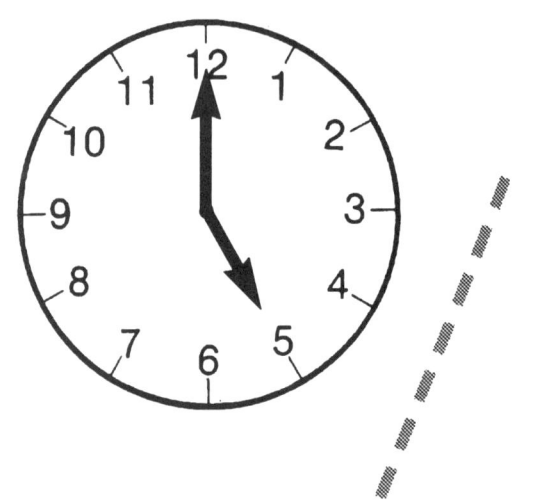

1 o'clock

3 o'clock

5 o'clock

7 o'clock

9 o'clock

11 o'clock

Parents: Explain to your child that time is written in a special way. Show the examples on this page, then have your child write the correct time.

What time is it?

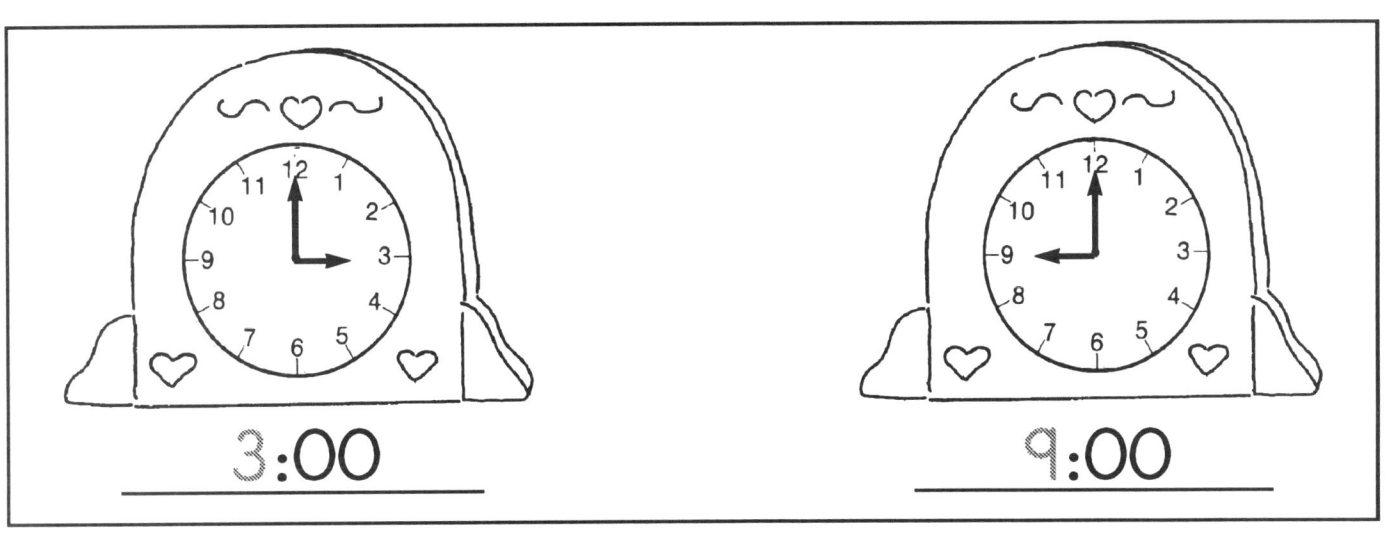

3:00   9:00

____:00   ____:00

____:00   ____:00

Write the time.

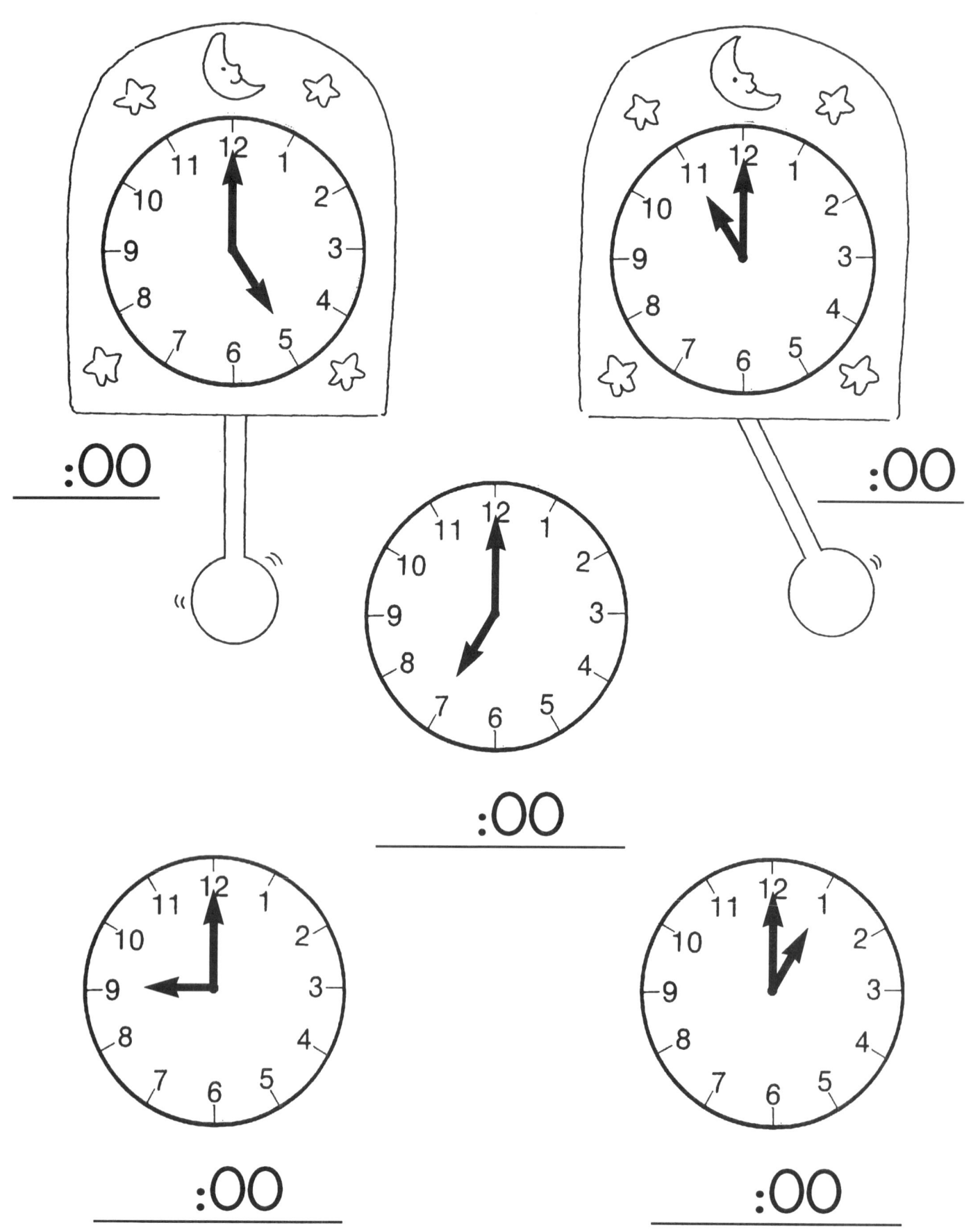

Write the numbers on the clock.

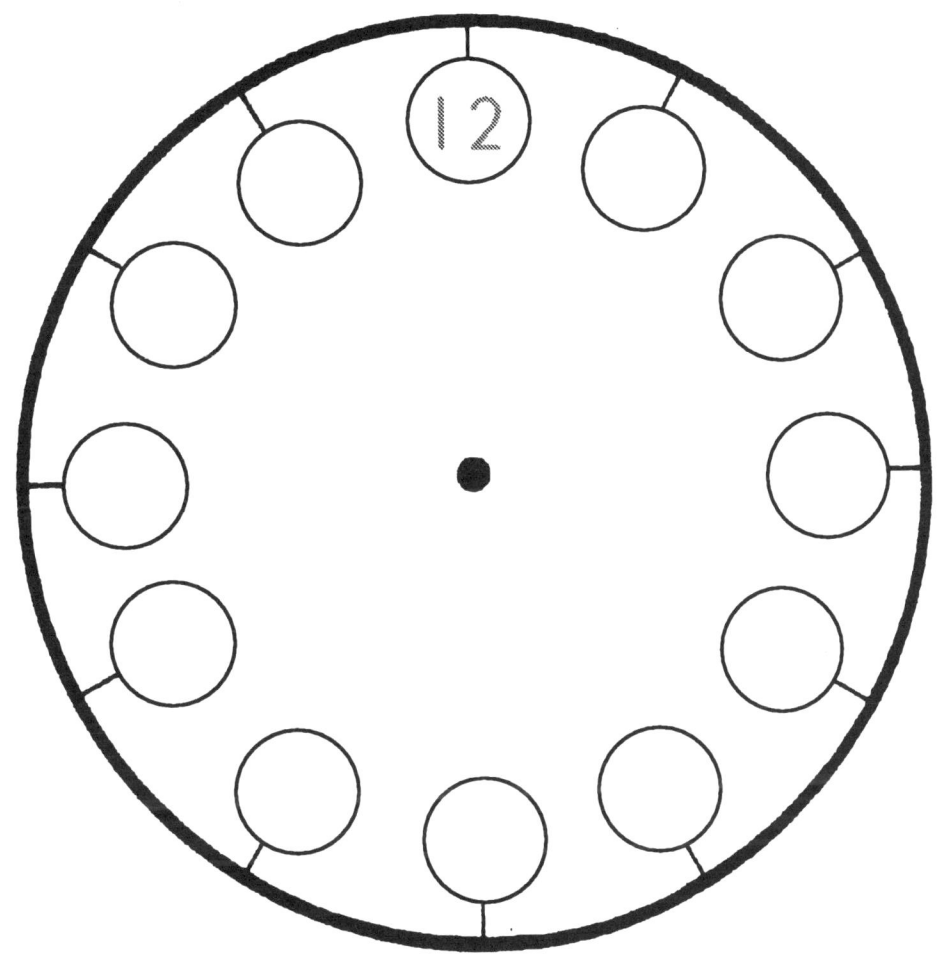

What time is it?

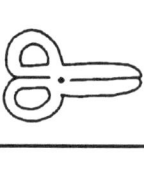 

paste	paste	paste
8:00	2:00	11:00
paste	paste	paste
5:00	7:00	3:00

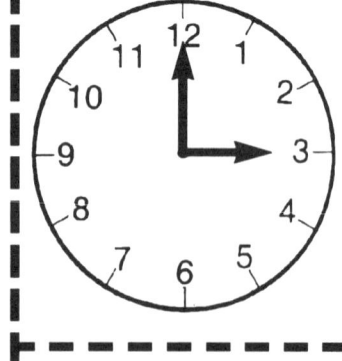  

  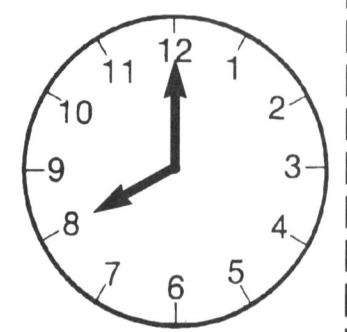

Parents: This page requires your child to draw the hour hand on the clock. If he/she has trouble, show how it is done.

Draw The Hour Hand.

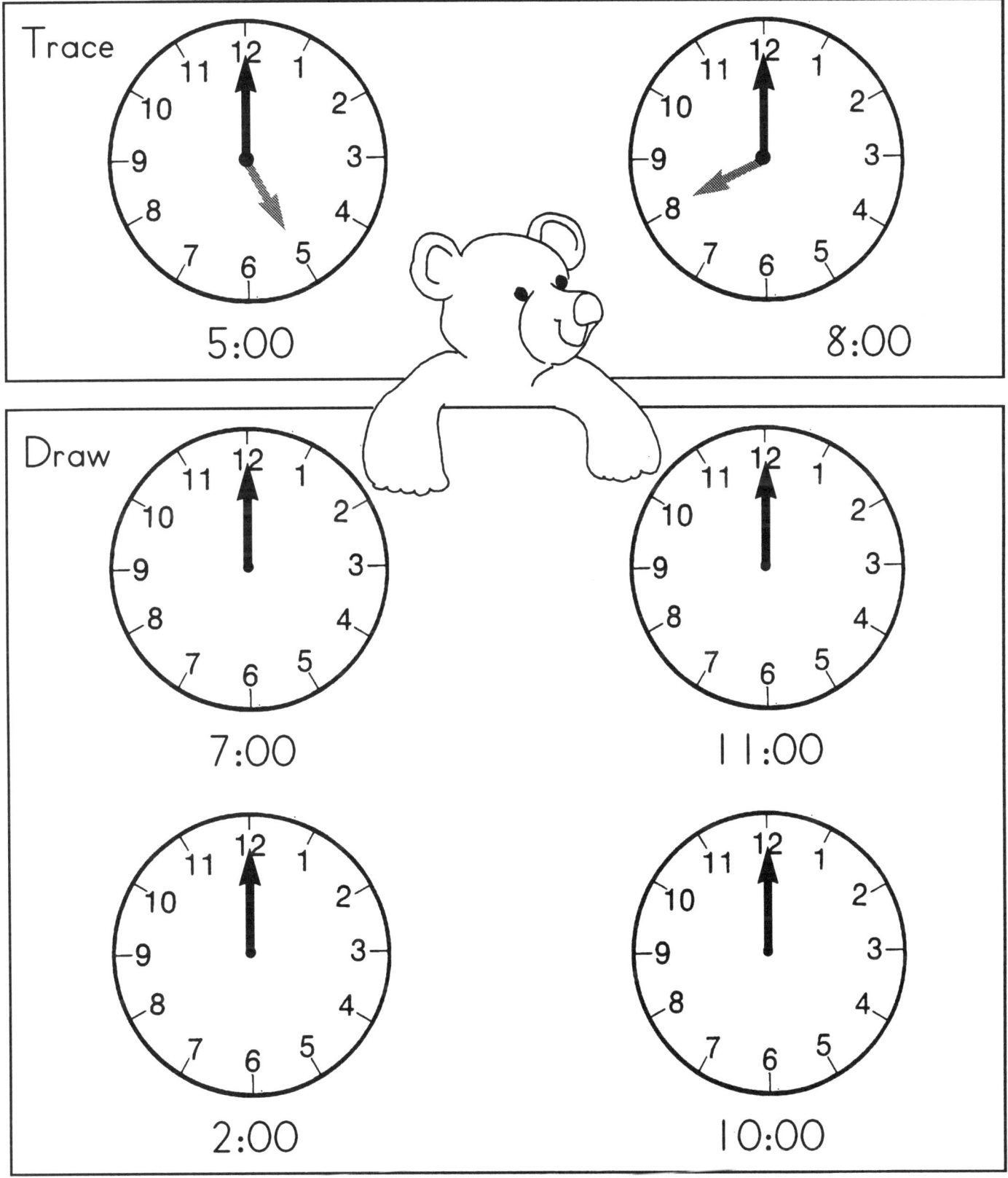

Parents:

Use the paper plate clock to show how time changes. Put a time on the clock and say "Now it is 3 o'clock ." In one hour it will be 4 o'clock ." Repeat this several times showing different hours.

Give the paper plate clock to your child. State a time. Have your child show that time on the clock. Then have him/her show what time it will be in one hour.

Repeat this several times, then have your child fill in this chart.

In One Hour

now	in one hour
6:00	___:00
4:00	___:00
1:00	___:00
9:00	___:00
11:00	___:00

Parents: Certain times are tricky to read when you are just learning. Show your child how the hands look on a clock at 6:00 and at 12:00.

6 o'clock or 12 o'clock?

Draw on the hands.

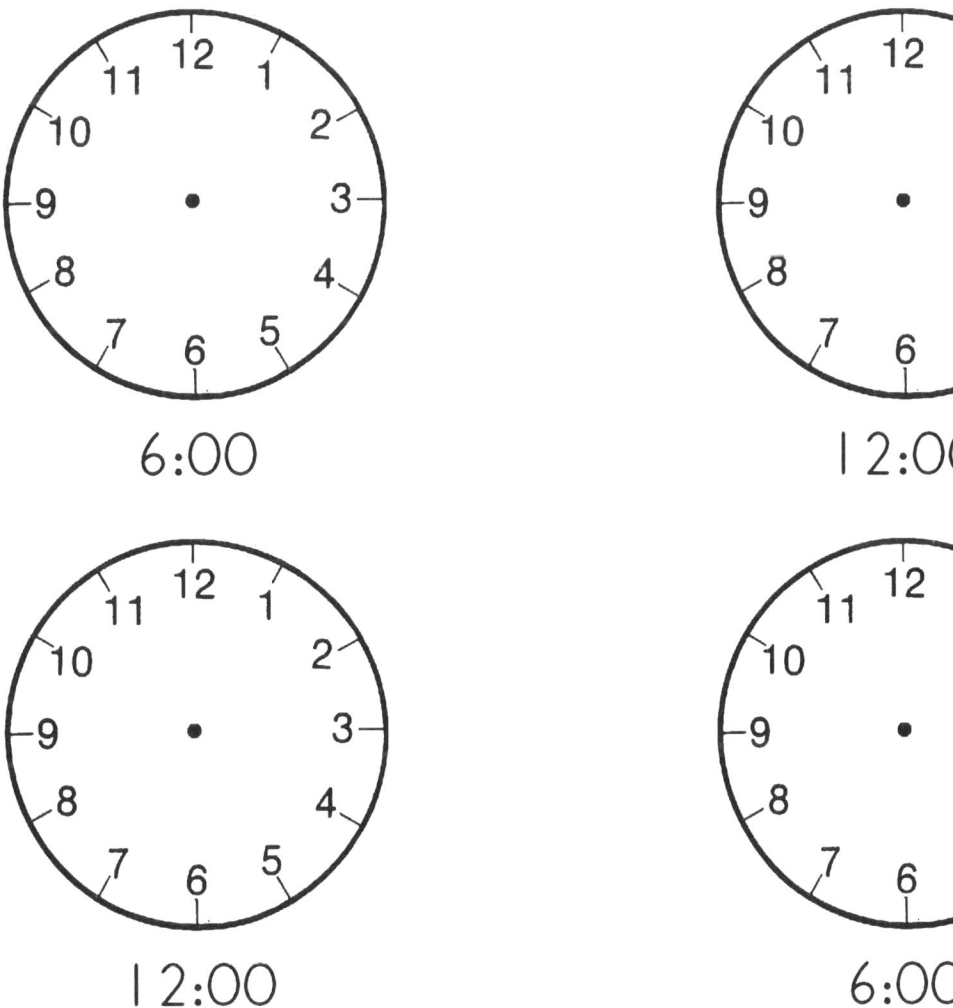

Parents: Help your child keep this chart for one day. Choose any day your child is not in school. As much as possible, stop each hour to have your child read the hour and write down what he/she is doing. If your child is not writing, have him/her draw a picture instead.

What I Did Today

Half-Past the Hour

Parents:

When your child is comfortable reading time to the hour, use the paper plate clock to show where the big hand is when it is a half hour (on the six).

Show where the hour hand is (between two numbers). Explain that you say "half past" and give the number.

Have your child move the minute hand to the six. Then have him/her move the hour hand half-way past a number and tell you the time. Prompt your child to say "It is half-past ___(time)___."

Repeat the activity several times, then have your child look at these clocks and tell you the time.

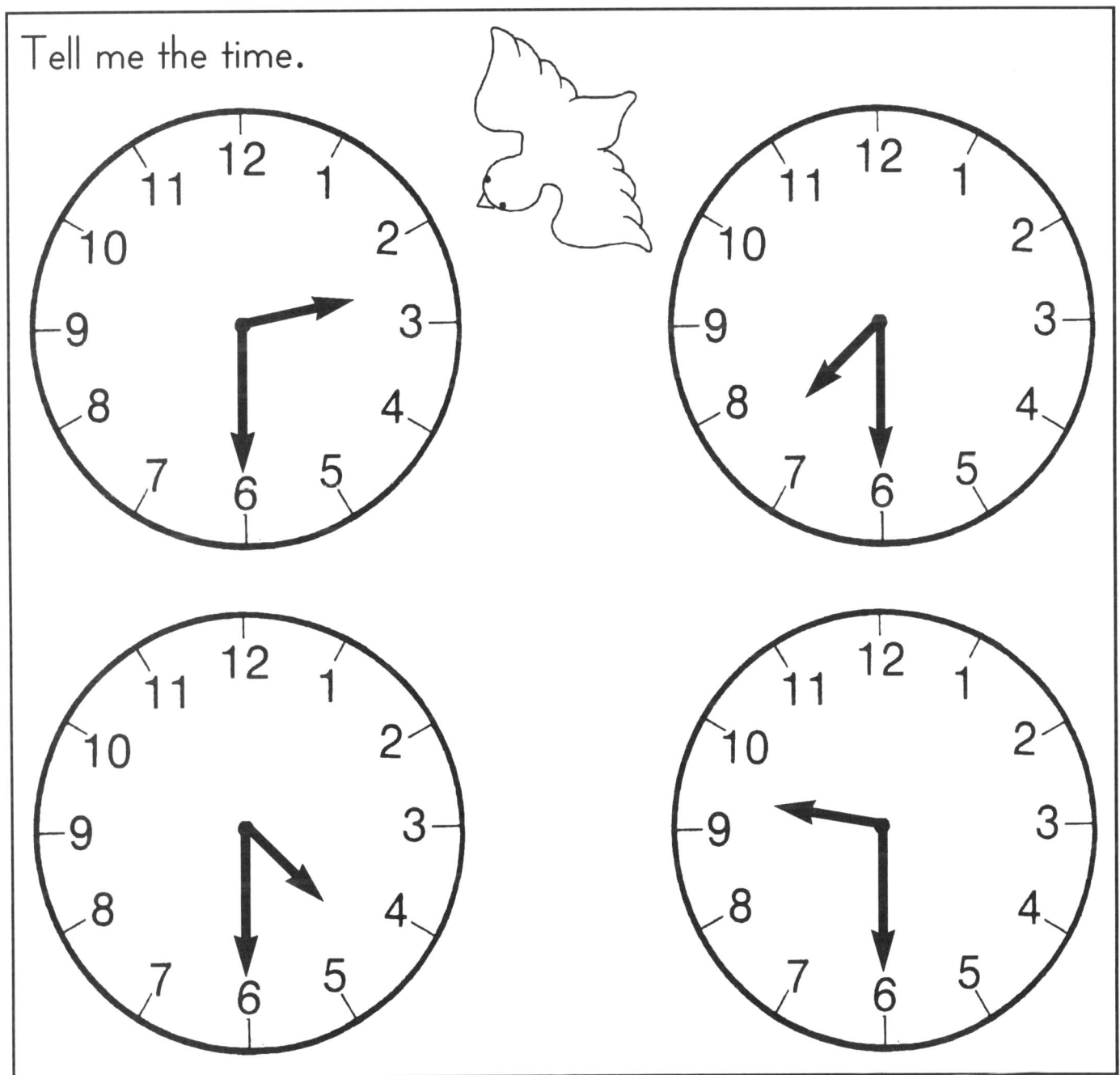

Parents: Explain to your child that there is another way to say a time like "half-past four." We can also say "4:30." They both mean the same time.

Fill in the Time

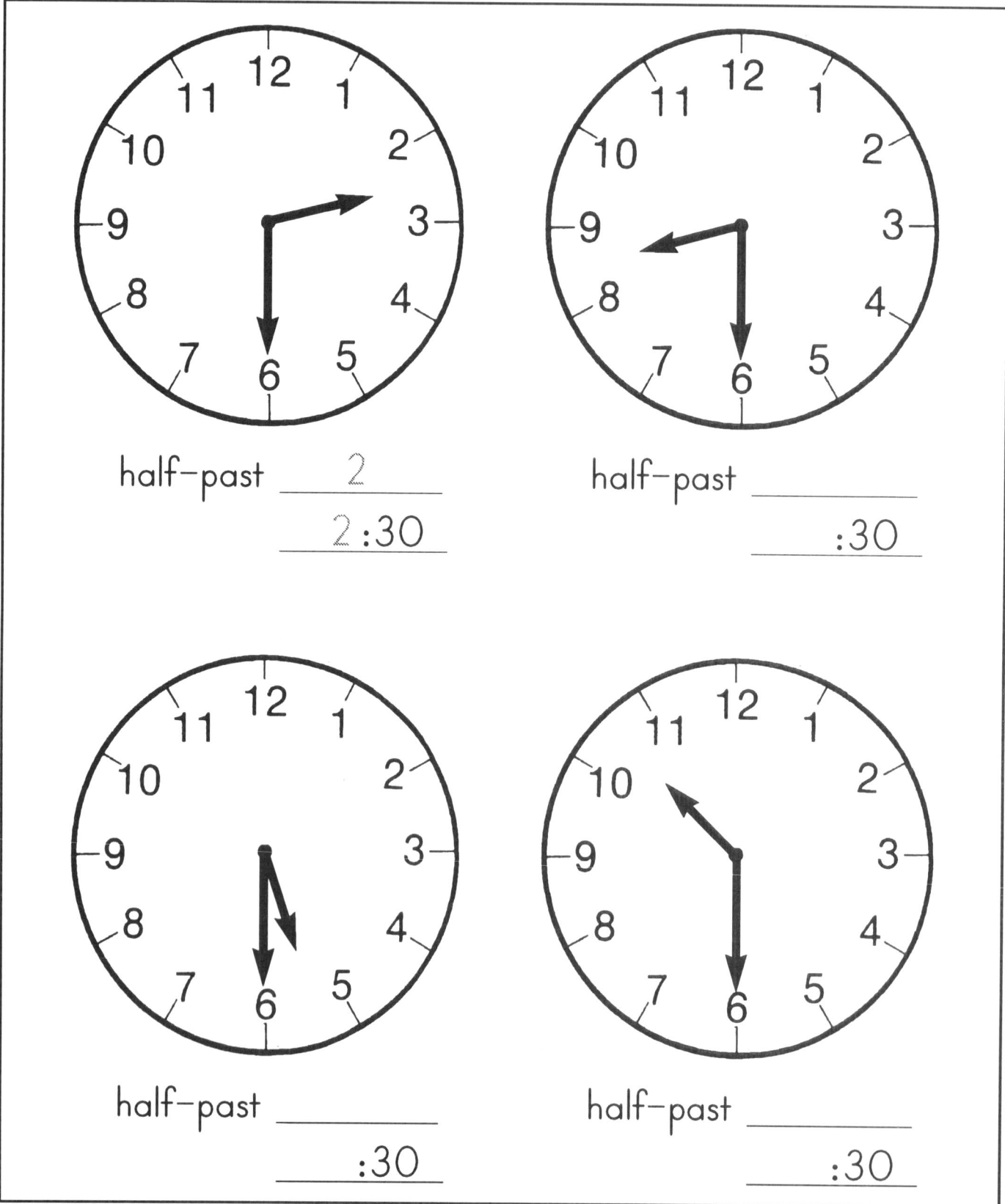

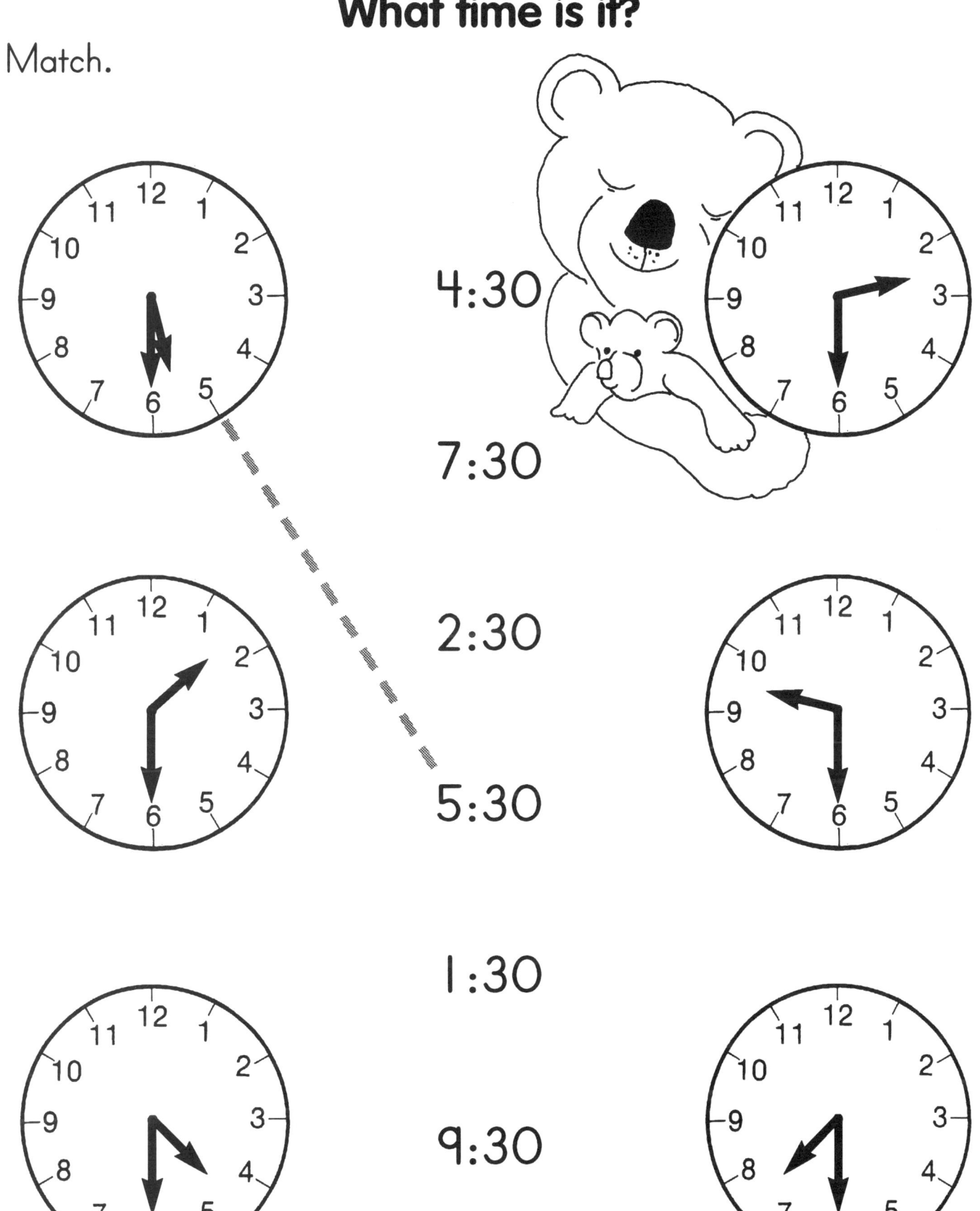

Parents: Explain to your child that clocks some in two different kinds. Some use hands (traditional), others show the numbers (digital).

Two Kinds of Clocks

Match:

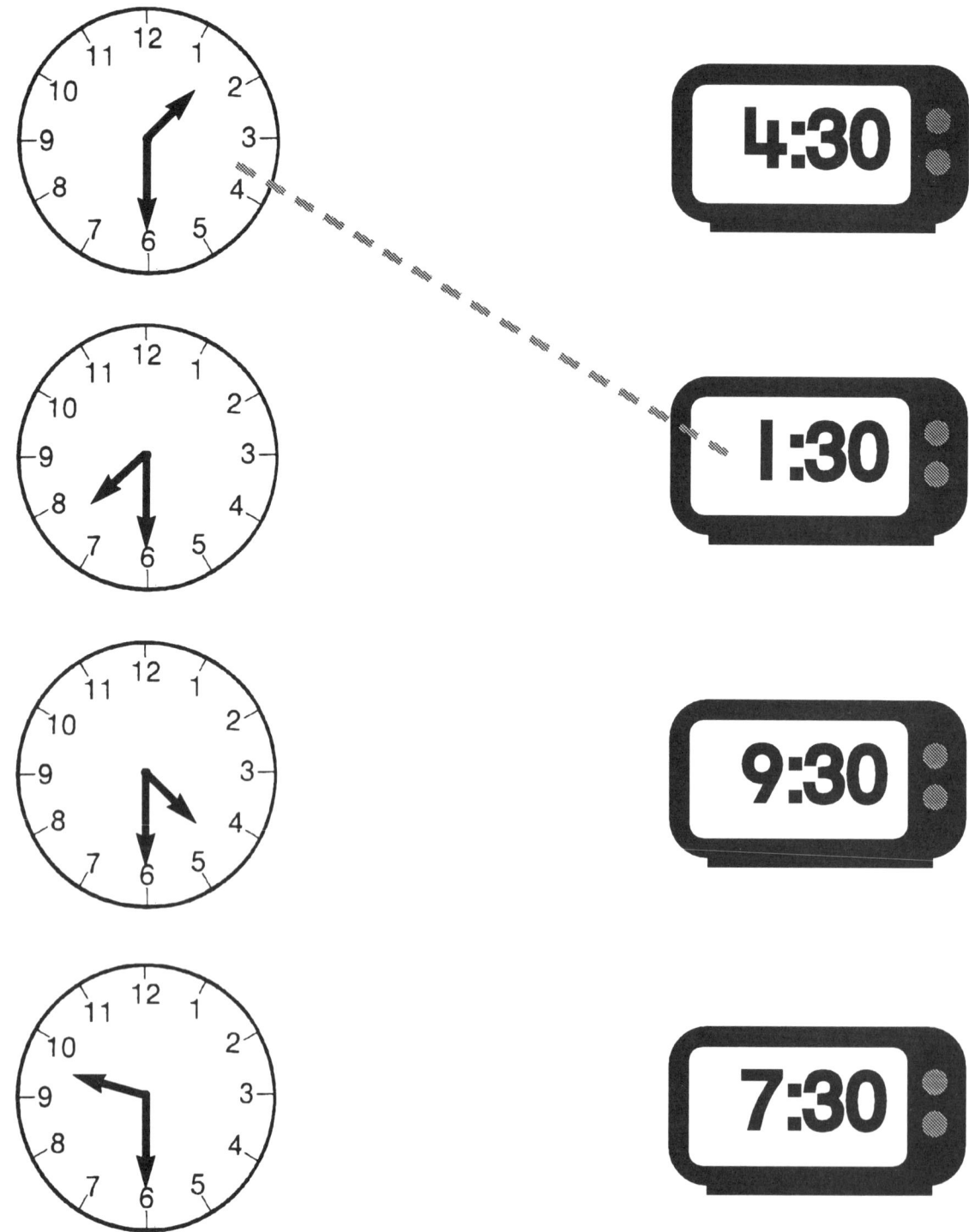

Where does the little hand go?

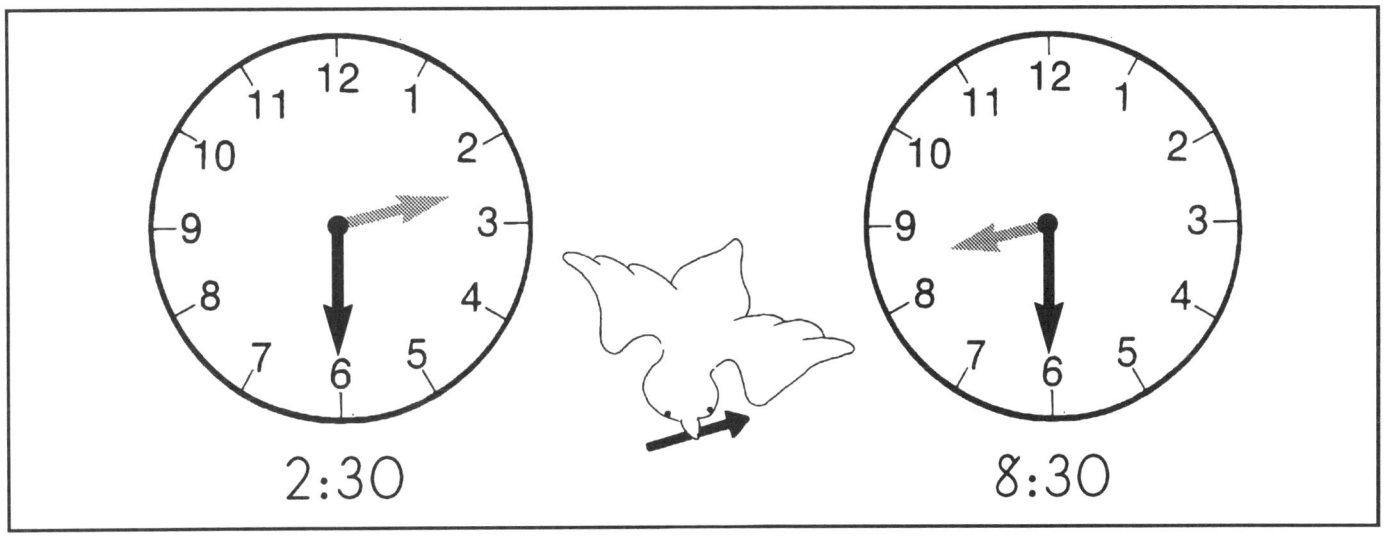

2:30   8:30

3:30    7:30

9:30    4:30

Half-past the Hour

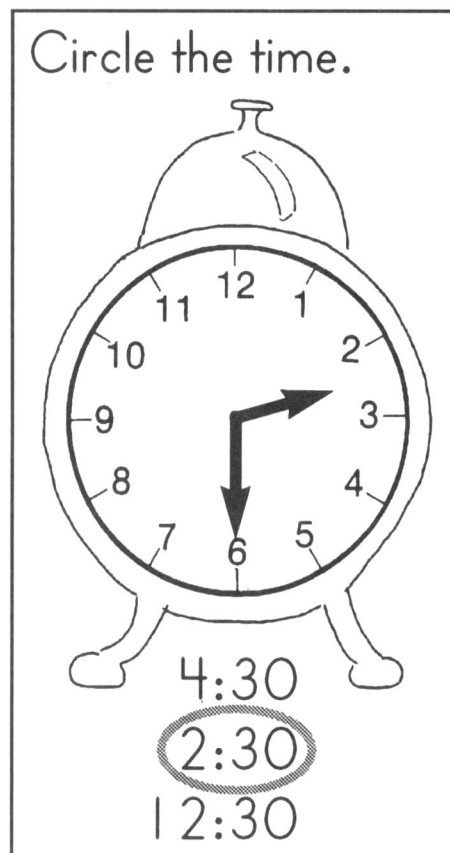

Circle the time.

4:30
(2:30)
12:30

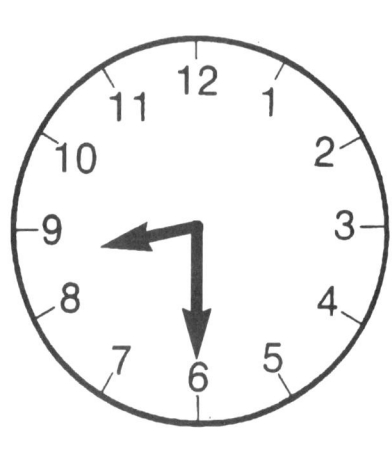

8:30
11:30
7:30

2:30
4:30
7:30

6:30
3:30
10:30

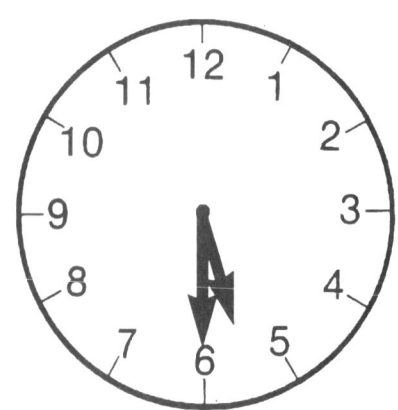

5:30
8:30
4:30

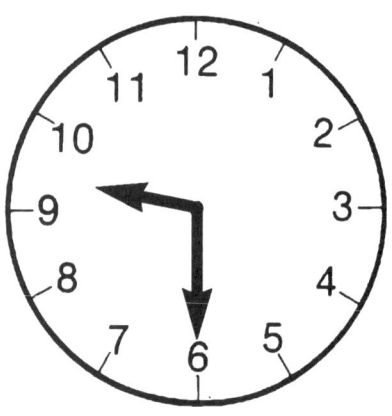

3:30
9:30
8:30

What Time Is It?

Circle the time.

Clock 1 (pocket watch):
9:30
(4:30)
6:30

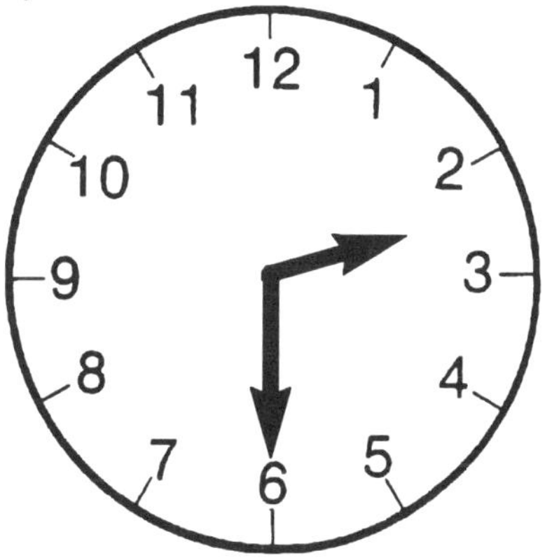

Clock 2:
2:30
7:30
1:30

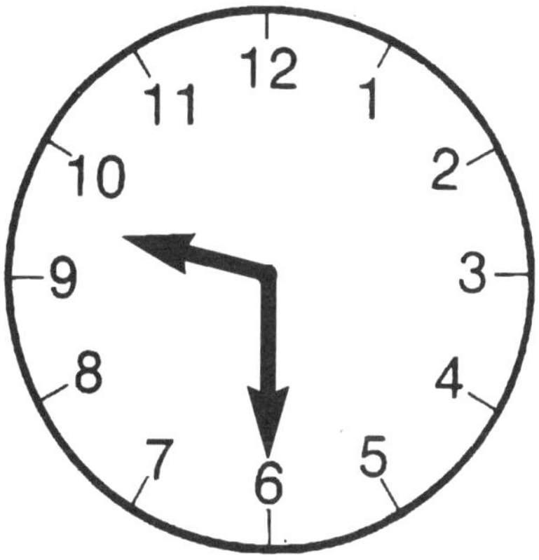

Clock 3:
8:30
5:30
9:30

Clock 4:
7:30
2:30
4:30

Clock 5:
10:30
9:30
11:30

Clock 6:
12:30
5:30
1:30

What time is it?

Match.

8:30

1:00

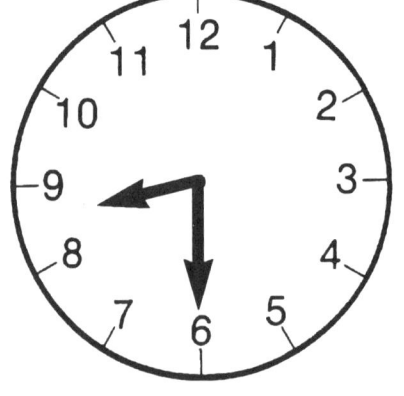
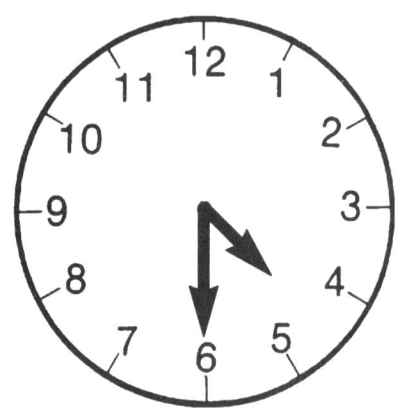

4:30

5:00

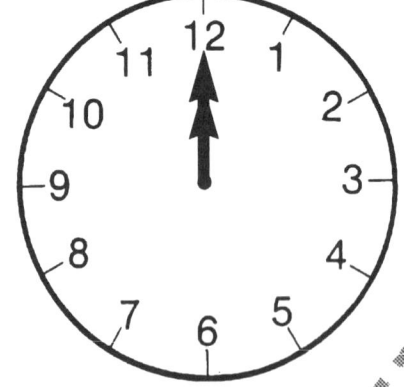

2:30

11:30

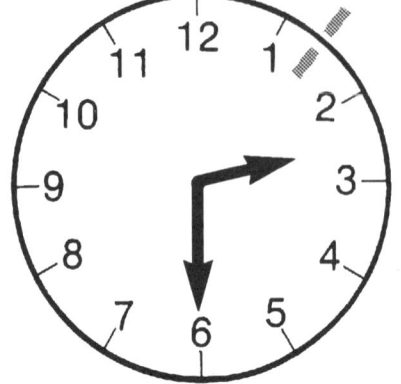

6:00

12:00

What time is it?

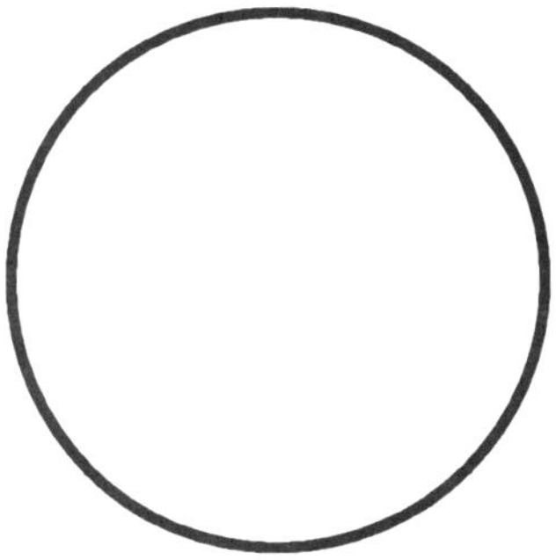

○	○
6:00	12:00
○	○
6:30	12:30

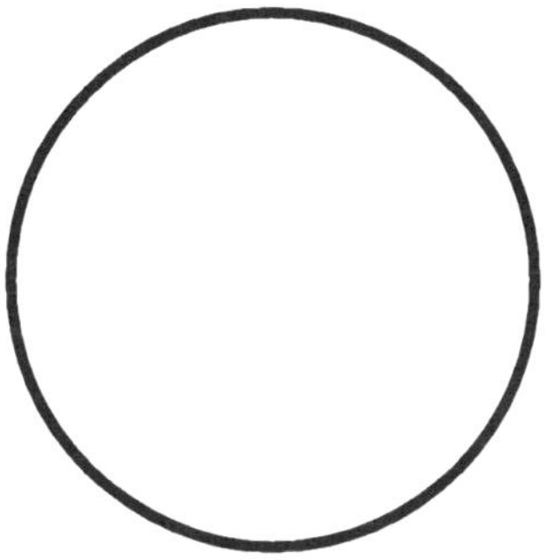

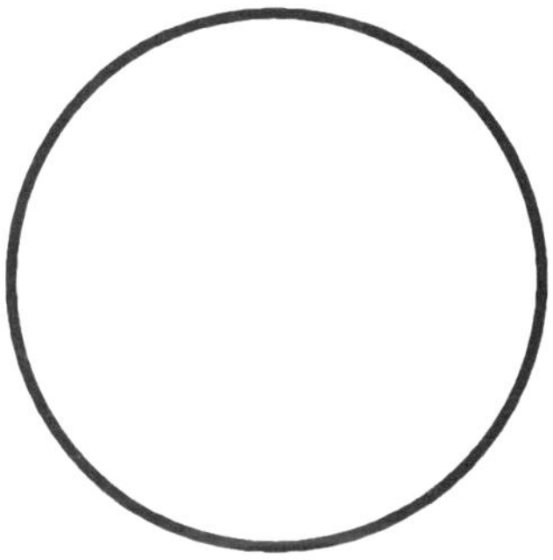

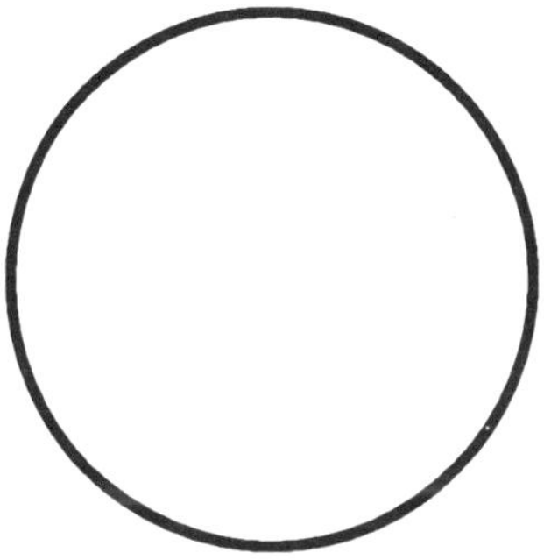

Put the hands on the clocks.

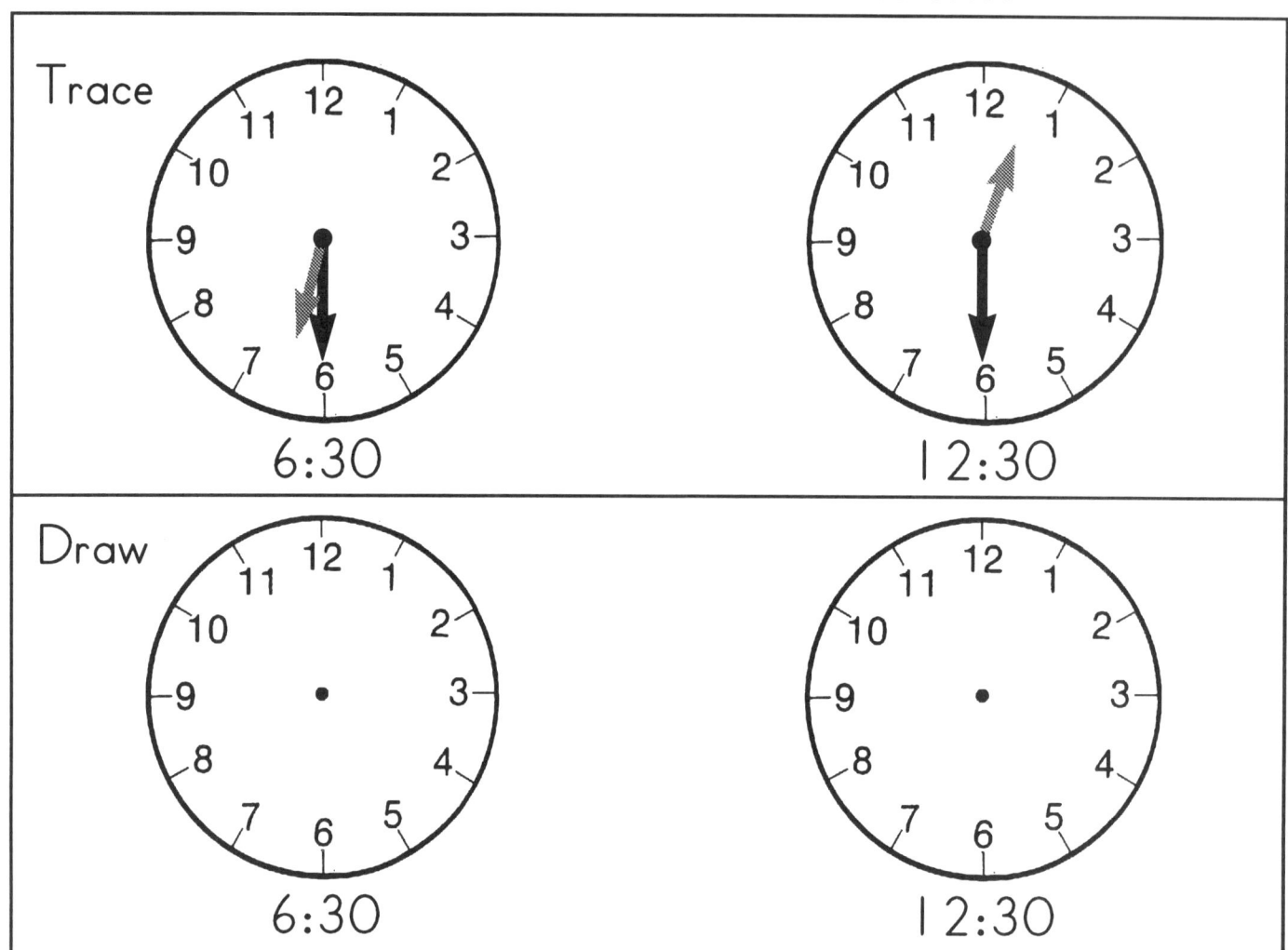

Match the Clocks

  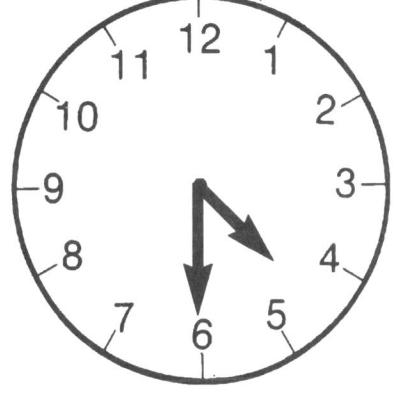

Parents: Help your child fill in the times on this bedtime chart. Keep the chart for one week.

Day	_____'s Bedtime Chart *childs name* Time
Saturday	(clock)
Sunday	(clock)
Monday	(clock)
Tuesday	(clock)
Wednesday	(clock)
Thursday	(clock)
Friday	(clock)

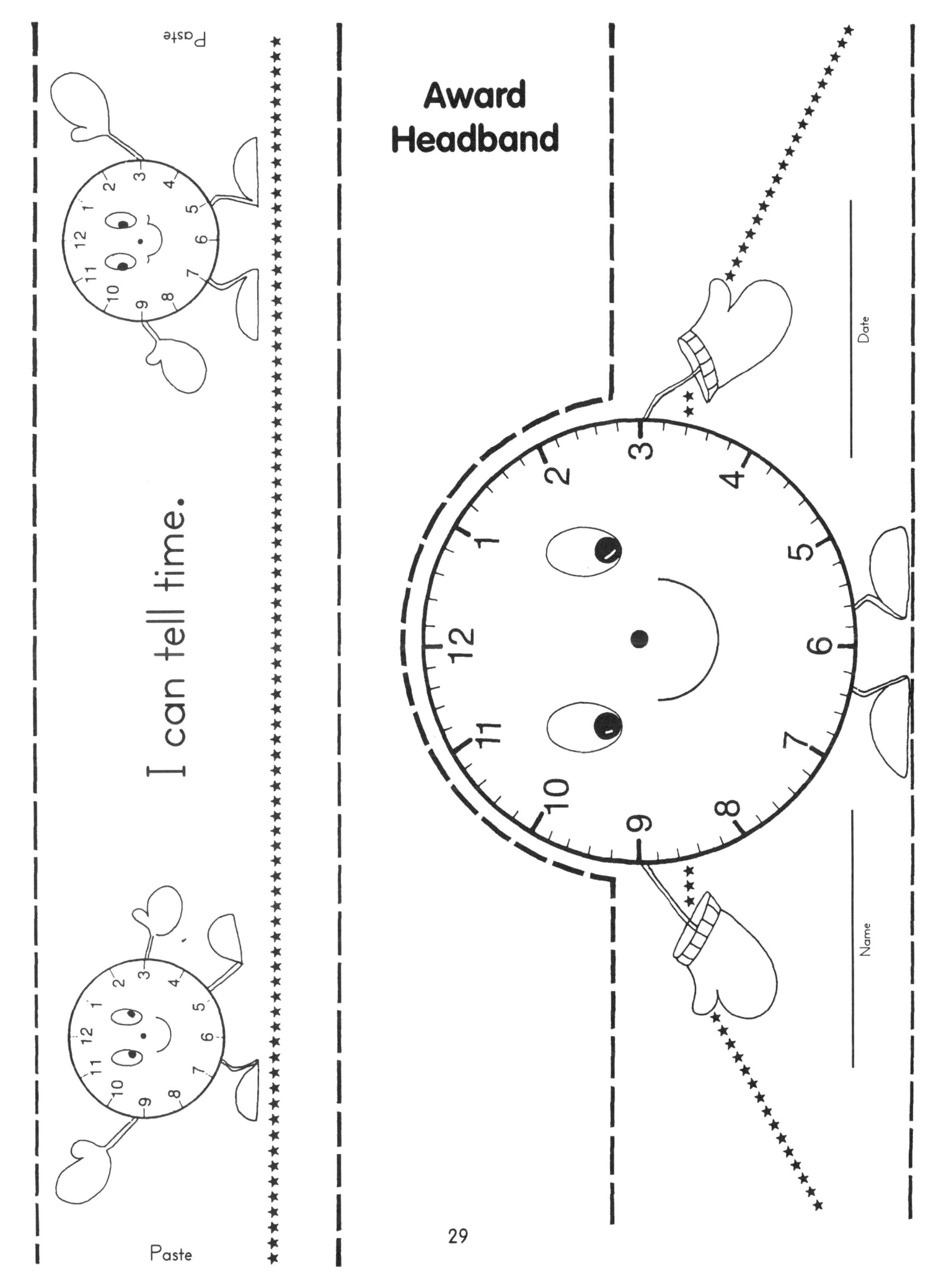

Answer Key

Please take time to go over the work your child has completed. Ask your child to explain what he/she has done. Praise both success and effort. If mistakes have been made, explain what the answer should have been and how to find it. Let your child know that mistakes are a part of learning. The time you spend with your child helps let him/her know you feel learning is important.

page 5
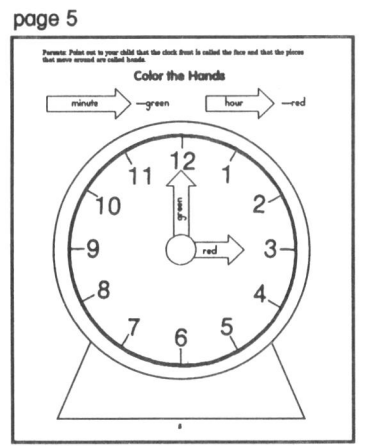

page 7
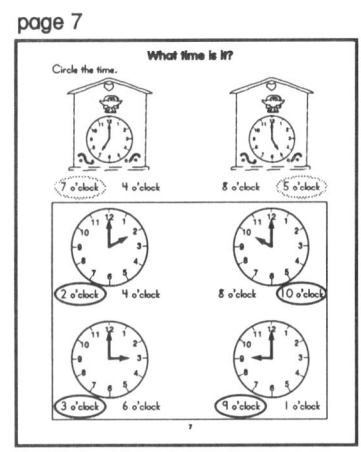

page 8
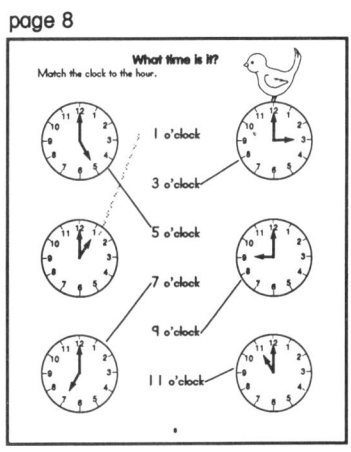

page 9
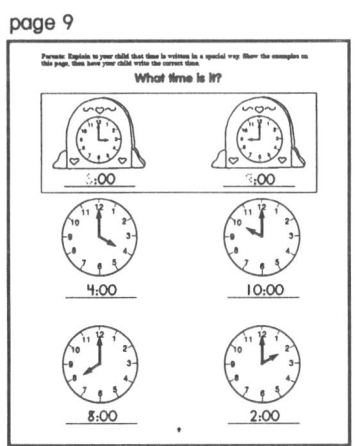

page 10
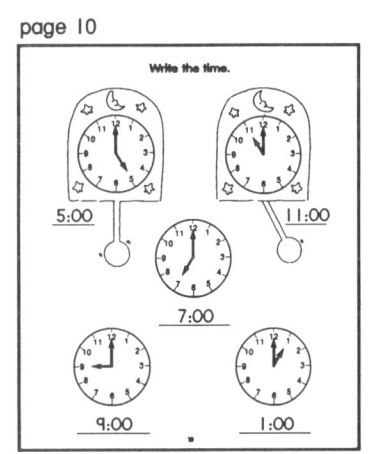

page 11
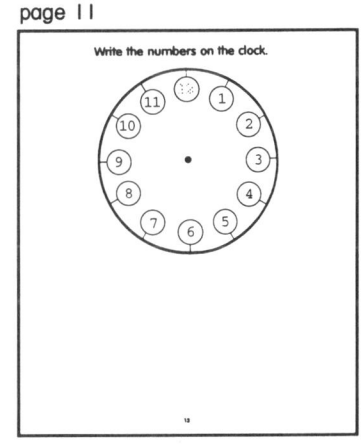

page 12
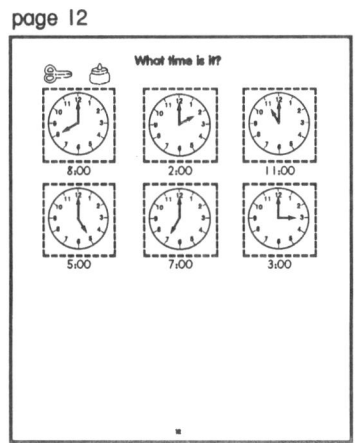

page 13
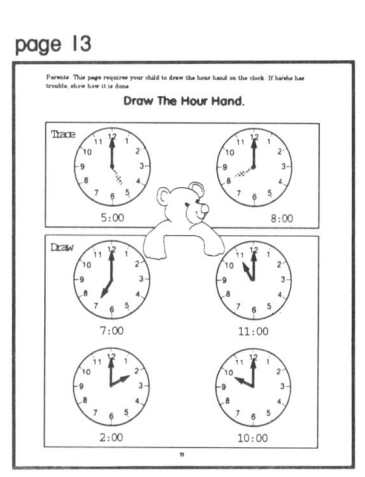

page 14
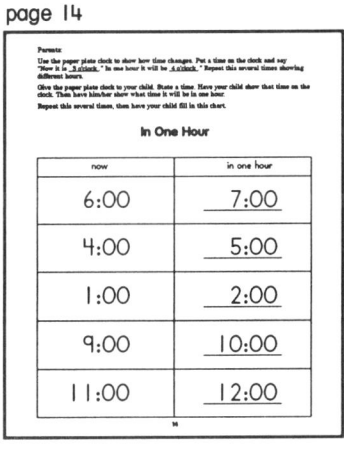

page 15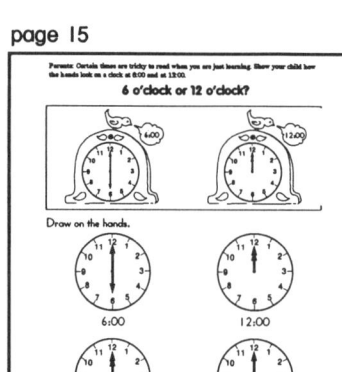

page 16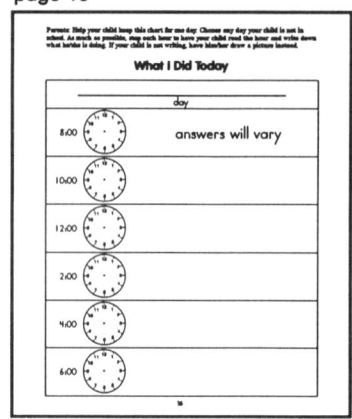

page 18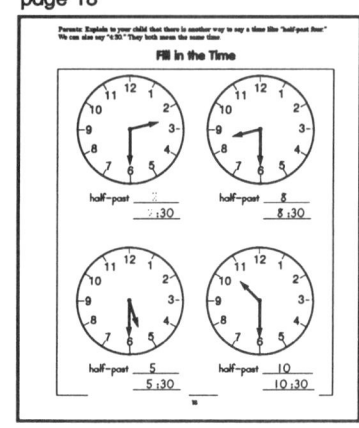

page 19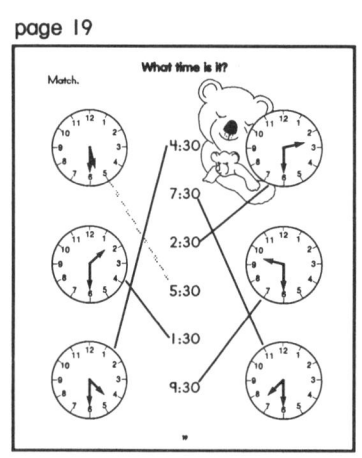

page 20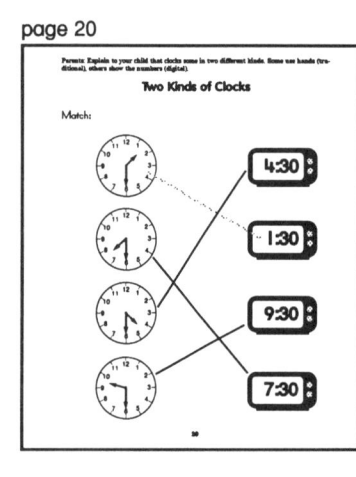

page 21

page 22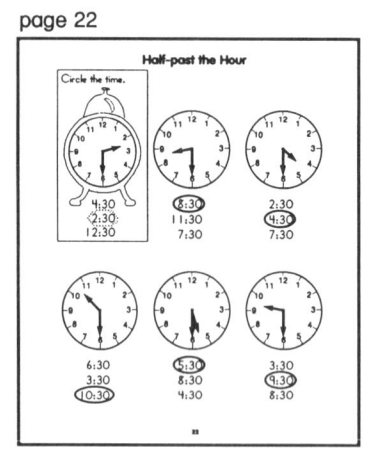

page 23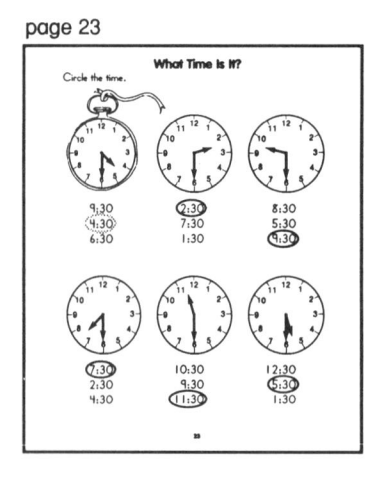

page 24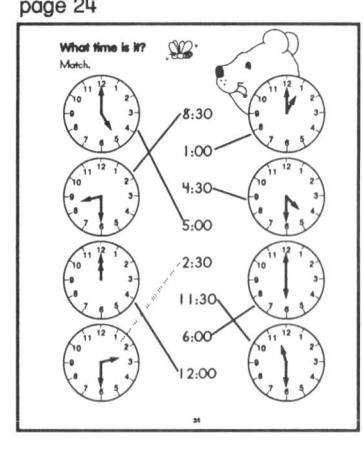

page 25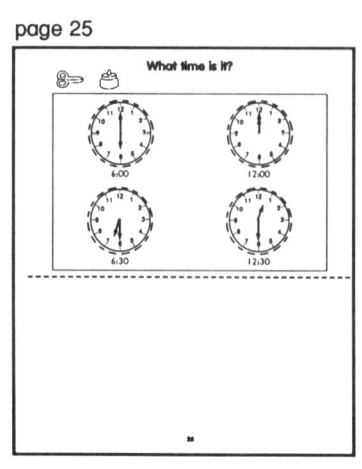

page 26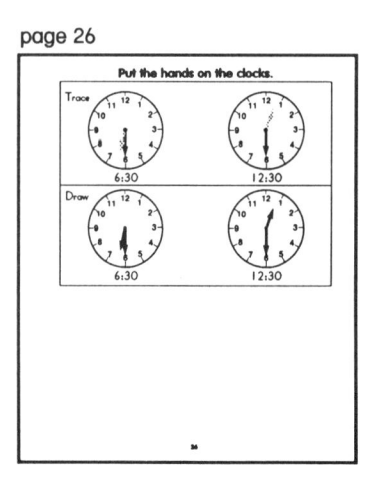

page 27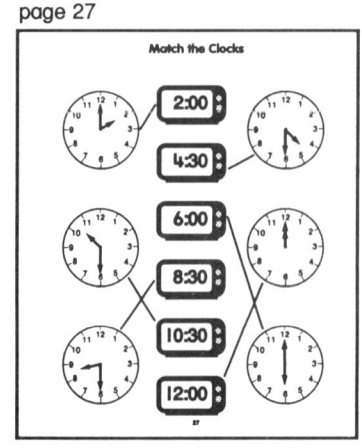